How To Meditate

Learn How To Meditate Step By Step And Reap The Benefits Of Meditation Everyday + Tips On How To Meditate Better

FREE DOWNLOAD

Sign Up For My Email List And Get The Ultimate Inner Peace Affirmation Audio Series To Attain Nirvana and Greater Peace for FREE!

Click here to get started: www.mikemccallister.com/list

Author's Note

Companion Animal Psychology

Thank you again for downloading this book!

Writing and speaking about the importance of inner peace and mental wellbeing has been closest to my heart, ever since 2017, when I lost my father. So much so, if there could be a point in time to see a sudden change in me, that would be it. Living in different continents and trying to get home in time as fast as a plane could go did not help. Unfortunately, I did not make it in time. I could not say my final good-bye. And I could not have all the conversations I thought of coming back to later.

The death of my father triggered a series of events in my personal life which not only affected my personal and professional relationships but shook me to the core leading to anxiety and panic attacks. As a result, my corporate poster boy rank was soon taken away and I was left to be a nobody which took its toll further.

Getting back was not easy. It took months of counselling, meditation and mindfulness to make peace with myself and others. But it was worth it. Along this journey my outlook on life changed. I realized that material pleasures are important but inner peace and mental wellbeing is priceless. And so, I began writing this series to help others chase the right things in life.

Also By Mike McCallister

Click here for my body of work: www.mikemccallister.com/books

- Steps to Finding Inner Peace and Happiness - How to Find Peace and Happiness Within Yourself (Buddha on the Inside Book 1)

- How To Meditate: Learn How To Meditate Step By Step And Reap The Benefits Of Meditation Everyday + Tips On How To Meditate Better (Buddha on the Inside Book 2)

Thank you, and good luck!

© Copyright 2020 - All rights reserved.

This document is geared towards providing exact and reliable information in regards to the topic and issue covered. The publication is sold with the idea that the publisher is not required to render accounting, officially permitted, or otherwise, qualified services. If advice is necessary, legal or professional, a practiced individual in the profession should be ordered.

- From a Declaration of Principles which was accepted and approved equally by a Committee of the American Bar Association and a Committee of Publishers and Associations.

In no way is it legal to reproduce, duplicate, or transmit any part of this document in either electronic means or in printed format. Recording of this publication is strictly prohibited and any storage of this document is not allowed unless with written permission from the publisher. All rights reserved.

The information provided herein is stated to be truthful and consistent, in that any liability, in terms of inattention or otherwise, by any usage or abuse of any policies, processes, or directions contained within is the solitary and utter responsibility of the recipient reader. Under no circumstances will any legal responsibility or blame be held against the publisher for any reparation, damages, or monetary loss due to the information herein, either directly or indirectly.

Respective authors own all copyrights not held by the publisher.

The information herein is offered for informational purposes solely, and is universal as so. The presentation of the information is without contract or any type of guarantee assurance.

The trademarks that are used are without any consent, and the publication of the trademark is without permission or backing by the trademark owner. All trademarks and brands within this book are for clarifying purposes only and are the owned by the owners themselves, not affiliated with this document.

Table of Contents

Introduction 10

Chapter 1: The Basics of Meditation 12

    What Meditation Is (And Is Not) 12

    How Meditation Works 14

Chapter 2: Science-Backed Reasons To Meditate 19

    Why Leaders Across the World Need to Meditate 25

    Who Should Meditate? 27

Chapter 3: The Best Time to Meditate (And Why) 29

    In the Morning 30

    Before Meetings and Important Tasks 32

    After Completing Work 33

    When Stressed 33

    During Lunch Time 34

    Before Going to Bed 34

Chapter 4: A Step-by-Step Meditation Guide 36

Step #1: Prepare 36

Step #2: Settle in 37

Step #3: Breathe Deeply 38

Step #4: Tune and Check-in 38

Step #5: Scan.. 39

Step #7: Watch.. 40

Step #8: Set it Free 41

Step #9: Progress 42

Step #10: Carry it With You... 42

Chapter 5: Meditation Techniques For Different Goals 44

Mantra Meditation to Boost Confidence, Peace, and Happiness... 44

Square Breathing Meditation For Stress Relief and Improved Focus 46

12-Minute Kundalini Yoga Meditation For Brain Power ..47

Conclusion 50

Introduction

At times, especially when it seems like obstacles are the only thing around us, life can become so challenging that focusing on your goals, and moving forward with clarity becomes a struggle.

In such moments, you ought to have at your disposal tools and strategies that can help make every process, journey, and endeavor meaningful and enjoyable for you. **Meditation** is one such tool. It primarily focuses on improving your sense of purpose, wisdom, clarity, focus, peace, and meaning in life.

Ajahn Brahm, a renowned British-Australian Theravada Buddhist monk, once said,

"Meditation is like a gym in which you develop the powerful mental muscles of calm and insight."

Meditation helps exercise your mind so that it becomes powerful and robust while maintaining its flexibility. By unlocking and harnessing its true potential, you can achieve all your goals.

If you would like to discover more about meditation, what it does, how it works, and how to reap its bountiful benefits, this book is for you.

In the pages that follow, you will learn everything you need to learn about meditation, including actionable tips and meditative techniques you can use to make meditation a constant in your everyday life. Every passage you read and page you turn will breed in you the interest and motivation needed to make meditation a routine practice.

Start reading this guide today to learn how to use meditation to unlock and embrace a truly remarkable life.

Chapter 1: The Basics of Meditation

Many of us often complain about the chaotic nature of our inner spirit, how challenging life is, or how we cannot focus on or accomplish our goals.

While most of these concerns are legit, when we complain, we become forgetful of the fact that the present moment is the only thing we have. What's more; we can use our present to overcome any challenge.

Meditation is about connecting with, living in, and using this moment, the now, to experience a more profound life experience. This chapter aims to give you a closer look at the science of meditation so that you can have a better idea of what the practice entails:

What Meditation Is (And Is Not)

Contrary to popular misconception, meditation is not about tunning into a new, different, or improved version of yourself or alternate universe where everything is 'just dandy.' The practice is primarily about *awareness training* and then using that awareness to cultivate a healthier perspective towards life.

Meditation is a useful tool that you can use to tap into and harness the full power of your thoughts to cultivate increased clarity, profound focus, and genuine happiness.

Meditation does not ask you to turn off your feelings or thoughts. A meditation session is not a lesson in shunning or disregarding your thoughts. All meditation asks you to do is to observe everything, your thoughts included, without attaching to it any labels, judgments, or ill feelings. By doing this, you gradually learn to understand everything better.

We have 50,000-70,000 thoughts every day, many of which are about similar ideas, concerns, fears, and problems. Of these thoughts, some are pertinent to our important goals, aspirations, and purpose in life.

To enhance your life experience, you need to learn how to discern essential thoughts from the nonessential ones and focus on the former so that you can understand them and yourself better. Developing this ability helps you let go of unnecessary, stressing thoughts; become more creative, and use the power of your thoughts to actualize all your goals. It helps teach your brain how to remain focused and attentive, which enables you to cultivate the peak performance you need to have to thrive on any task.

Dr. Ron Alexander, a successful psychotherapist and author of the book, *Wise Mind, Open Mind,* believes that your mind's strength, which consists of your efficacy, resiliency, and emotional quotient, arises as you learn to control your mind. Your mental strength is undoubtedly and arguably one of the most empowering tools you can build and use to improve every aspect of your life.

To use meditation to build mental strength, you need to understand how it works:

How Meditation Works

Meditation works by targeting and then improving the functionality and regularity of brainwaves.

Humans have five main categories of brainwaves, each of which corresponds to a different set of activities. Meditation allows you to move from a high-frequency brainwave to a lower-frequency brainwave.

Lower-frequency brainwaves have slower wavelengths; slower wavelengths create more time and space between thoughts. When you experience more time between thoughts, it allows you to choose which thoughts to invest your energy in and what corresponding actions to take.

The creation of space between thoughts is why you feel calmer and more focused after engaging in consistent meditation. This happens because meditating relaxes the racing mind, which keeps your mind from jumping from one branch of thought to the other.

The 5 Brainwave Categories

Below are the five brainwaves your brain functions in and their related functionalities in daily life:

1. ***Gamma State:*** This brainwave has a frequency range of 30Hz-100Hz. It corresponds to a state of active learning and hyperactivity and is the most suitable time to absorb and retain information. Educators and trainers often encourage audiences to jump up and down or pace around because doing so activates this mental state and increases the chances of permanently assimilating information in the brain. However, the over-stimulation of this brainwave state results in chronic stress and anxiety.

2. ***Beta State:*** This state has a frequency range of 13Hz-30Hz. We function in this brainwave state most of the day. This state powers our alert state of mind and is active when we are thinking about something, analyzing things,

planning our work, assessing and categorizing information. An overstimulated beta state leads to anxiety.

3. ***Alpha State:*** This state has a frequency range of 9Hz-13Hz. The brainwaves start slowing down when you enter this state and exit the active thinking state of mind. Once you enter this brainwave state, you start feeling more peaceful, grounded, and calmer about yourself and life in general. The alpha state is the state your brain functions in when you are taking a quiet stroll in the woods, having a relaxing yoga session, or doing anything that helps you unwind. When you are in this brainwave state, you are reflective and lucid. You also have a somewhat diffused sense of awareness.

4. ***Theta State:*** This brainwave state has a frequency range of 4Hz-8Hz. It becomes active when you start meditating actively and regularly. When you get into the theta state more often, your verbal and actively-thinking mind transitions into a more visual and meditative mind. You shift from the actively planning mind and move to a more profound state of consciousness. This, in turn, improves your intuition and helps you reflect on and establish a vivid nexus between things and make informed decisions.

5. **Delta State:** This brainwave state has a frequency range of 1H-3Hz; getting into this state comes after years of profound meditation. With that said, you can use meditation to unleash this state of mind in the short-term, provided your meditation quality is excellent. In this very alert and wakened phase, you experience an enlightened state of mind that helps you understand everything clearly.

You need each of these five brainwave states at different times and instances in life. Overstimulation and under-activation of any of these five states can cause chaos, confusion, and problems such as depression, anxiety, stress, and even physical health problems.

To live a meaningful, empowered, and prosperous life, you need to trigger the right state at the right time and promote a better sense of awareness. That is where meditation comes in handy.

Meditation helps remove irregularities in the five brainwave states. It equips you with the power to switch on the right brainwave state at the right time by focusing on one thought, one emotion, one feeling, and one moment of life at a time.

Now that you have a better understanding of what meditation is, what it does, and how it works, move on to the next chapter where we shall explore the reasons why you should meditate.

Chapter 2: Science-Backed Reasons To Meditate

Lama Surya Das, an American lama of the Tibetan Buddhist tradition, a chant master, poet, author, meditation teacher, and spiritual activist once beautifully said:

"With every breath, the old moment is lost; a new moment arrives. We exhale, and we let go of the old moment. It is lost to us. In doing so, we let go of the person we used to be. We inhale and breathe in the moment that is becoming. In doing so, we welcome the person we are becoming. We repeat the process. This is meditation. This is renewal. This is life."

Meditation teaches us to let go of everything that has happened so that we can embrace every new moment that unfolds with increased clarity, acceptance, and a nonjudgmental attitude. This unique ability brings forth many positive improvements in our life.

Let us look at science-backed reasons why we need to meditate and why meditation is a must-engage in practice for everyone:

#: Sharpens your attention

Meditation improves and sharpens your attention, which helps you concentrate better. It reduces mind-wandering, thus allowing you to pick one thought from a cluster of many and focus on it attentively.

Many of us experience a racing mind, aka monkey state of mind, which is a state where our mind continually jumps from one branch of thought to another, unable to stick to one thing at a time.

Naturally, when you rush through thoughts and tasks, you cannot focus sharply on anything, which in turn compromises your ability to analyze information and effectively solve problems.

Meditation resolves the problem by improving your ability to filter insignificant things from significant ones, which allows you to focus on the latter and solve issues creatively[1]. Studies[2] show that the increased attention induced by meditation lasts

---

[1] http://journals.plos.org/plosone/article?id=10.1371/journal.pone.0036206

[2] https://www.ncbi.nlm.nih.gov/pmc/articles/PMC3132583/

for approximately five years, even after you stop meditating regularly.

#: Improves resiliency to mild and chronic stress

Every time you confront a challenge or a problem, your brain triggers the stress response, also called the 'fight or flight' response.

Activation of this state results in different physiological changes such as rapid breathing, increased heartbeat, and various other changes that help the body cope with the stressful situation outside. This response is essential because it enables you to manage problems and ensures your survival.

With that said, if tiny issues cause you to feel stressed out, you are likely to suffer from mild to chronic stress that keeps you from living a healthy, happy life. Meditation proves itself a valuable ally by reducing the intensity of your stress, helping you calm down during tensile situations.

Neuroscientific research shows that meditation dampens the activity in your amygdala[3], the area of the brain in charge of

[3] https://www.ncbi.nlm.nih.gov/pmc/articles/PMC4666115/

regulating the stress response. Additionally, meditation improves the connection between your prefrontal cortex and the amygdala, which helps your mind mitigate stress better.

#: Makes you more compassionate

Studies[4] on meditation have shown that regular meditation sessions, especially those that help you focus on fostering love and compassion towards others, can help you nurture a compassionate, gentle heart. Meditation does this by lessening the activity in your amygdala during situations involving suffering; at the same time, it activates circuits in your brain that promote feelings of love.

As you nurture compassion, you become a kinder human being who spreads love and positivity into the world. Being this kind of person improves your personal and professional relationships.

A study conducted on meditation in 2016 examined the positive effects of the practice on 88 couples. Researchers examined their cortisol levels before and after conflict situations. They observed that compared to those with a low level of mindfulness, those who practiced meditation

---

[4] https://www.ncbi.nlm.nih.gov/pmc/articles/PMC3713090/

regularly had higher levels of mindfulness and were able to return to normalcy quickly after a conflict.

This shows that regular meditation helps strengthen bonds with loved ones and enhances your ability to live a happy, meaningful life.

#: Improves your mental health

A meta-analysis conducted in 2014 and later published in the JAMA Internal Medicine Journal showed the effect of a mindfulness meditation program on 3,515 participants. The results proved that meditation reduces anxiety, stress, and depression, and improves mental health.

Researchers concluded that this happens because meditation helps calm down the unusually active gamma and beta states, and triggers the alpha and theta states when needed. Activation of the latter brainwave states calms down the racing mind and promotes body and mind relaxation.

#: Helps you become unbiased and nonjudgmental

A study determined that meditating on loving and kindness based suggestions reduces prejudices towards homeless people. A related study[5] illustrated that the mindfulness induced by meditation eliminates unconscious bias most have towards the colored and elderly.

Meditation helps improve your perspective towards things, which ensures that you nurture a more aware, accepting, and healthy sense of understanding. Cultivating this sense enables you to perceive things for what they are and develop a nonjudgmental attitude that allows you to accept everything and everyone as they are in the moment of experience.

#: Improves your physical health

Studies also show that meditation has a positive impact on physical health, more so in the sense that it improves conditions such as high blood pressure, diabetes, and cardiovascular problems.

Moreover, meditating regularly also helps reduce joint pains, backaches, headaches, and digestive issues. Regular meditation strengthens your heart, brain, and immune

[5] https://www.researchgate.net/profile/Bryan_Gibson2/publication/294276984_Brief_Mindfulness_Meditation_Reduces_Discrimination/links/570baaf508aee06603519a68.pdf

system. Meditation also helps unlock your creative abilities, enables you to think outside the box, and improves your cognitive skills and level of happiness.

For these reasons, and because of the pure sense of tranquility that meditation induces, we need to make meditation as a must-engage in practice that we carry out every day:

Why Leaders Across the World Need to Meditate

While everyone must meditate, leaders across the globe need to incorporate meditation in their everyday lives the most.

The world is currently going through a traumatic pandemic that has induced an intense sense of fear on everyone and turned cities and marketplaces that once teemed with people into deserted lands. In this time, we need leaders who can focus better on the problem and come up with unique solutions.

The modern world needs compassionate, innovative, optimistic and calm leaders who can act nonjudgmentally after thinking about the greater good. At such critical moments in human history, we need leaders who can find unique ways to manage and improve situations that threaten the human condition. Meditation can help leaders nurture these abilities, which is why they must practice it daily.

Steve Jobs, a renowned world leader in the field of IT, once said this about meditation:

> *"You start to see things more clearly and be in the present more. Your mind just slows down, and you see a tremendous expanse in the moment. You see so much more than you could see before."*

If you want to enjoy a perspicuous, healthy sense of perspective that helps you live a truly empowered life, meditation is the way to go about it.

Who Should Meditate?

While anyone and everyone can and should meditate, the practice is particularly ideal for the following people:

- People who experience chronic stress, anxiety, and depression; meditation can give such people massive relief from these problems

- People who usually experience a racing state of mind and cannot focus on thoughts and tasks effectively

- People who have big dreams and goals that they wish to fulfill

- World leaders who wish to accomplish great objectives and inspire their followers

- People who wish to gain better clarity

- Anyone and everyone who wants to enjoy a higher degree of self-awareness and explore their genuine desires better

- People who are going through relationship and want to foster love and care in their relationships.

- Anyone who is experiencing spiritual problems and has a strong desire to foster better self-connecting

- Anyone who aspires to unlock a profound state of mindfulness and live every day with deep meaning and happiness.

If you fall in any of these categories, or if you want to equip yourself with the power to live life with clarity, meditation is for you.

Since you now know why you should meditate, let us discuss the best times to meditate.

Is this book helping you in some way? If so, I'd love to hear about it. Your honest reviews would help readers find the right book for their needs and help me tailor the future books to yours. Reviews are the single most important factor in determining if a book succeeds, so I'm incredibly thankful for people like you who I can rely on to leave one.

Click here to leave a review for this book on your favorite online store: www.mikemccallister.com/books or click here to leave a review on Goodreads: www.mikemccallister.com/goodreads

Chapter 3: The Best Time to Meditate (And Why)

Baba Ram Dass, an American psychologist, author, and spiritual teacher, once said:

> *"Meditation and concentration are the way to a life of serenity."*

At this point, you have a clear understanding of how meditation induces mindfulness and clarity in your life, and how these states pave the way for a magical, serene experience.

Now we shall discuss the best times to meditate and the reasons why you should meditate at those times.

In the Morning

Meditating after waking up is a brilliant way to start your morning with inspiration, positivity, calmness, and focus.

Often, after waking up, we check our phone and email for messages. Once we do that, we get trapped into a series of tasks that never end. If that's what you do now, you are likely to start your day in a rush, which may explain why you feel swamped in the morning, when what you should feel is fresh after a refreshing night's sleep.

When you introduce meditation into your morning routine, even a short meditation session of 5 minutes, this situation changes.

Mornings are usually a time of day when you are likely to have fewer worries orbiting your mind and can, therefore, meditate with better focus. If you meditate at this time, you relax your mind and create space for positivity and wisdom.

Moreover, practiced as part of your morning routine, meditation energizes and soothes your nerves, giving you the right amount of zeal, optimism, and inspiration to achieve all your targets for the day.

If you are new to meditation, getting an app pertinent to the exercise is a good idea to get started with it.

Calm[6] and Headspace[7] are free, meditation-based apps that make it easier for you to begin and get settled with the practice.

---

[6] https://www.calm.com/

[7] https://www.headspace.com/

Before Meetings and Important Tasks

We often feel biased towards action before major tasks and meetings. During such times, we need mindfulness and peacefulness the most, which is why it is a good idea to meditate for a few minutes before an important meeting or task.

Meditating at such a time helps you take note of your emotions, soothe strong ones, and gain clarity on the meeting/task so that you can execute it with enthusiasm.

Moreover, meditating shortly before engaging in critically-important tasks, particularly meetings that involve thorough briefing to team members, can help you conduct the session with increased focus.

In such an instance, meditation will make it easier to listen to your team members, prep them properly, and listen to every input and suggestion with increased attention. Practicing this level of focus will ensure that the meeting moves forward smoothly; it will also be easier to motivate the team members to achieve the targets.

Similarly, meditating before conducting key activities and tasks such as giving a presentation, preparing a report, or anything else that is crucial to your performance and productivity. This is because it helps you focus well on the job and effectively avoid distractions.

After Completing Work

Meditating, at the end of the workday, perhaps before exiting the workplace or after getting home from work, is a good idea. If you have a physically or mentally demanding job, it is a wise idea to meditate after completing your work so that you can relieve the built-up tension and unwind.

Meditating, after completing work, creates a boundary between your work and personal life, which makes it easier to relax without worrying about any pending tasks. A meditation session practiced at the end of the workday helps you return home happy and ready to enjoy leisure pursuits and time with family.

When Stressed

Every time you feel stressed and notice yourself engaging in messy, unproductive thought patterns, take a few moments to breathe deeply and meditate.

Even a few minutes of calming meditation will create the much-needed space between your thoughts and give you the calmness you need to let go of unhelpful thoughts.

Simply plop into your chair, gently shut your eyes, bring your attention to your breath or any part of your body, and observe it peacefully. If you do that for a few moments, you'll unwind and destress.

During Lunch Time

Lunchtime hours can be an overwhelming time of the day because you have taken on a great deal of stress from your work assignments since the start of the day. You should use this time to relax and energize yourself to keep up with the remaining work. Meditating at this hour can be very soothing because it loosens you up and prepares you for the next few hours of work.

Before Going to Bed

Meditation helps you slow down and break-free from stressful and negative thought patterns that often keep you from sleeping comfortably at night. You can get the best sleep by meditating for 30 to 60 minutes before bedtime. When you meditate before getting into bed, it lightens you up and prepares your mind for relaxation and sleep.

To cultivate the habit of meditating routinely, begin by doing it in the morning, and then infuse short meditation sessions into other times of the day.

Since now you know the best time to meditate, let's discuss a step-by-step method you can use to meditate and enjoy its benefits.

Chapter 4: A Step-by-Step Meditation Guide

Meditation is a simple thing to practice. If you take care of a few things and practice it consistently, you will be meditating easily in a matter of days.

Here is a step by step process you can use to get started with meditation and make it a habit:

Step #1: Prepare

Before beginning a meditation session, especially your first one, take care of the following practicalities:

- Choose a peaceful, clean, organized spot because a noisy, cluttered, and messy one shall be a distraction.

- Pick a time of day when no one or any other task will bother or distract you. Doing this will ensure that you can give the practice your undivided attention for at least 5-10 minutes.

- For a few weeks, stick to meditating at the same time of day so that your mind can create robust neural pathways that help you make the practice consistent and routine.

- Wear comfortable clothes that don't hug you too tightly and disrupt your focus during meditation.

- Having a stopwatch or timer will ensure that you don't need to glance at your watch/phone several times during meditation, thereby killing your attention and awareness.

- You can meditate by sitting on your yoga mat, chair, couch, or bed. Choose a sitting platform that compliments your level of comfort.

- Do not meditate at a time when you are feeling hungry; hunger pangs are distracting. At the same time, do not meditate on a full stomach because it can make you drowsy during the practice.

After taking care of these things, be in your meditative spot at the right time so that you can get settled.

Step #2: Settle in

Be in your meditation spot a few minutes before the start of your meditation time so that you can settle into your couch, chair, or yoga mat.

As you sit, keep your back straight, neck relaxed, and chin lightly tucked in. Get comfortable, and if sitting for 5 minutes feels uncomfortable, lie down on the floor or bed. Close your eyes, and keep your arms by your side. Relax by thinking of anything calming.

Step #3: Breathe Deeply

Take a deep in-breath through the nose and focus on it. Take another deep out-breath and exhale through your mouth; keep your attention on the process. Breathe in this manner for five breaths so that you can calm down, unwind, and gently tune into your body.

Step #4: Tune and Check-in

Check-in with your body and peacefully observe how you feel. Notice the sensations in places where your feet touch the ground or where your body contacts your sitting platform. Feel the weight of your body or your arms resting on your lap. Acknowledge any or all of your senses and pay attention to anything you can hear, smell, feel, taste, or see.

Take your time with each experience before moving on to the next one. If you smell something, focus on it for a few moments and then observe a texture you want to feel.

Step #5: Scan

Very gently, turn your mind towards your body and run an in-depth scan, starting at the top of your head down to your toe.

As you do this, observe any discomfort, tension, or uneasiness in any part of the body and take note of it without trying to change it. Scan your body again, but this time, pay attention to the parts of the body that feel relaxed. Dedicate 20 to 30 seconds to every scan.

After scanning and observing your body a few times, turn your awareness to your thoughts and calmly observe them. Notice your thoughts and acknowledge each of them, one after another. Do not attempt to change them; just watch them as calmly as possible.

Gently turn your attention to your underlying mood and acknowledge it without being judgmental of it. If you do not observe anything unsettling, you do not need to probe further. Be consciously aware of any sensation, movement, or any thought you observe, and calmly stay with it before moving onto another element.

Reflect on the 'Why'

After the first 2 to 3 minutes, take a 30-second pause; use the break to think about why you are sitting and meditating.

Recognize any kind of desire or expectation you may have, and gently let it go by turning your focus on how good it feels to be calm now. Since those moments are not part of your present, try not to worry too much about how this calmness will help you in the long run.

Meditation is about tuning into the moment and nurturing mindfulness of the present, which can only happen when you settle into and fully embrace the here and now. To settle in, tell yourself to sit peacefully and calmly, without worrying about anything else.

After reflecting on your 'why' for a few moments, bring your attention to your breath.

Step #7: Watch

Do not make any conscious effort to deepen or make your breath longer: just breathe naturally in your usual manner. Direct every ounce of self-awareness to the observance of your breath as it moves in and out of your body.

Notice where you can sense your breath; perhaps you feel it robustly at your shoulders, belly, chest, or anywhere else. Focus on how your breath makes you feel within, the time you take to inhale and exhale, how calm or stressed you feel, and the likes.

During this process, you will wander off in thought. When that happens, count your breath, and very patiently, align your thoughts with your breath. You may need to do this a few times, so be patient with yourself, but stick to the practice. After a few sessions, you will get the hang of it.

Step #8: Set it Free

For about 30 seconds, do not observe your breath, body, senses, or anything else; instead, give your mind the freedom to wander freely. Let it drift off to wherever it wishes to go, but make sure you focus on one thing at a time.

Setting your mind free helps you become comfortable with being one with, and at peace with the present moment. Use this prompt to progress gently towards the end of the practice:

Step #9: Progress

As your practice nears its end, turn your awareness to physical feelings.

Become aware of the surface upon which you sit, how your feet contact the floor, how your hands feel in your lap or by your side, and other such elements. Notice everything you can touch, hear, or smell.

When the timer beeps, or when you feel ready to exit the practice, open your eyes with as much gentleness as you can muster.

Step #10: Carry it With You

Before you exit the practice and get back to your routine chores, develop a clear idea of the task you intend to engage in next. If you want to make tea, dress up for work, or use the washroom, create a vivid mental image of it.

Carry the awareness you just created during the meditation session to the next undertaking, and from there, onwards to the next task in line. By doing this, you will stay aware throughout the day, which will enhance your level of mindfulness.

As you navigate your day, look for moments you can use to reflect on what it feels like to have focused attention and clarity. For instance, when you sit to work, when having your first cup of coffee in the morning, or when taking the subway, take a few, relaxing, re-centering deep breaths.

If you practice these ten steps consistently, meditation will become more natural, and you will be able to meditate with a level of awareness that will ensure you take something meaningful from every meditation session.

In the next chapter, we shall discuss simple meditation techniques you can use to complement what you just learned:

Chapter 5: Meditation Techniques For Different Goals

What follows are simple but incredibly powerful meditation techniques. You can use them any time of day to achieve different goals such as increased peace, clarity, focus, happiness, and confidence.

Mantra Meditation to Boost Confidence, Peace, and Happiness

A mantra is a suggestion you chant several times (in one sitting or per day) so that it can imbed in your subconscious mind where it gets down to the work of rewiring your mental models/beliefs accordingly.

For instance, if you want to be happy, you can chant 'happiness' or 'I am happy' as you meditate on the mantra. The more you do this, the more affixed to your subconscious mind the mantra becomes, and the easier it becomes for your mind to create similar thoughts that it then sends out into the universe to attract experiences that bring you happiness.

Whether you want to nurture compassion, a loving attitude, happiness, peacefulness, confidence, or any other positive virtue, use mantra meditation for 2 to 10 minutes. In a matter of weeks, you'll accomplish the goal.

Here's how you can practice it.

- Get clear about what you want. Do you want to improve your focus, become more peaceful, boost your confidence, or become loving towards your partner?

- Create a short mantra centered on your goal. It could be a phrase or just one word. For instance, if you want to become calm, you could simply say 'peace.'

- If you are choosing a phrase, keep it under seven words and only use positive words that make you feel as if you have achieved your goal. For instance, to be happy, say, 'I am happy,' instead of, 'I want to be happy' or 'I will be happy.' Making sure your mantra is positive ensures that you give your subconscious the suggestion that you are happy right now, which helps you nurture mindfulness now.

- Settle into your meditation spot, set your timer, and close your eyes. Even if you are traveling in the subway, are in a lavatory, or out in the park, you can use mantra meditation.

- Take five deep breaths and then start chanting your chosen mantra. Chant it slowly and consciously so that you can focus on its vibration.

- Whenever your mind wanders off in thought, return your awareness to your mantra.

- If you feel pressed for time, chant your mantra for 2 minutes, but if you can meditate on it for longer (10+ minutes), the better off you will be for it.

After a single session, you will feel happier and lighter. When you carry out the meditation regularly, you will achieve your desired goal.

Square Breathing Meditation For Stress Relief and Improved Focus

To relieve anxiety and work with killer focus, try this quick square breathing meditation technique.

- Relax and tune into your body. You could be sitting in your meditation spot, or anywhere else.

- Close your eyes and breathe in through the nose to a count of 4.

- Hold the breath to another count of 4.

- Exhale through your mouth to a count of 4.

- Observe that out-breath for another count of 4.

- Doing this creates a square (of sorts).

- Carry out these steps at least 20 times, or for 5 minutes.

You will be amazed at how serene you feel within a few minutes.

12-Minute Kundalini Yoga Meditation For Brain Power

This Kundalini Yoga meditation improves your memory, focus, and enhances your overall cognitive faculties.

Here is how you can practice it:

- Sit comfortably and bring your gaze to your third eye, the place between your eyebrows.

- Practice the *Gyan Mudra*. A mudra is a hand and finger position that connects your fingers with different regions in your brain to produce specific effects. To practice the Gyan Mudra, keep your arms straight, with your hands resting on your knees. Let the tips of both the thumbs and index fingers touch gently.

- At this moment, chant 'saa,' which represents infinity, the start of time, and the cosmos
- Bring both the tips of the thumbs to the tips of the middle fingers
- Next, chant 'taa,' which stands for existence and life
- Gently bring the tips of the thumbs to the tips of the ring fingers
- At this point, say 'naa,' which signifies transformation, death, and change
- Now, bring your pinky fingers and the tips of your thumbs together
- Chant 'maa,' which stands for rebirth
- Chant every mantra for around 3 to 4 seconds
- Repeat this cycle for 11 minutes.
- Start with a regular, relaxed voice for 2 minutes; switch to a whisper for 2 minutes, and then chant silently for the

next 3 minutes. Return to the whisper for the following 2 minutes and practice with a loud chant in the remaining 2 minutes.

- As you engage in this meditation, visualize the energy of every sound you chant and feel it moving from the top of your head to the middle of your eyebrows.

- After you meditate for 11 minutes, release the mudra, keep your hands on the sides and simply sit in silence for a minute.

If you work on this practice daily, with time, you will become more focused, sharper, and mentally stronger.

Conclusion

You are amazing; it is about time you realized that. Harness that power and use it to build a peaceful life.

This book has equipped you with every strategy you need to achieve this goal. Now take action!

Did this book help you in some way? If so, I'd love to hear about it. Your honest reviews would help readers find the right book for their needs and help me tailor the future books to yours. Reviews are the single most important factor in determining if a book succeeds, so I'm incredibly thankful for people like you who I can rely on to leave one.

Click here to leave a review for this book on your favorite online store: www.mikemccallister.com/books or click here to leave a review on Goodreads: www.mikemccallister.com/goodreads

FREE DOWNLOAD

Sign Up For My Email List And Get The Ultimate Inner Peace Affirmation Audio Series To Attain Nirvana and Greater Peace for FREE!

Click here to get started: www.mikemccallister.com/list

Preview Of 'How To Be Mindful Of Thoughts: Steps To Achieving Mindfulness And Living In The Moment (Buddha on the Inside Book 3)'

A day has 24 hours (or 1440 minutes), but as you well know, time flies by so fast that many of us struggle to get things done, enjoy activities and just make the best use of our time. When many of us look back at the end of every day, we cannot pinpoint exactly what we did with our previous 24 hours. Indeed, time just seems and feels like it just flew by and we were onlookers who were not sure what was happening!

Yes, we are physically present in the moment and the tasks we do, but we are not emotionally and mentally invested in them. We lack what experts refer to as mindfulness, which, according to Jon Kabat-Zinn, a renowned professor of medicine and one of the pioneer researchers on mindfulness, causes a sense of forgetfulness. One of his most famous quotes on mindfulness states,

"Mindfulness means being awake. It means knowing what you are doing."

When you are truly mindful of yourself, and the present moment, you fully know how you feel, what you are doing, and how you do it. This very awareness has the power to change your life significantly, for good.

This book, How to Be Mindful of Thoughts is a complete mindfulness blueprint that walks you through the process and provides you with actionable and powerful ways to practice mindfulness and harness its power. It's concise, yet profound; simple, yet comprehensive and 100% beginner friendly. So, if you want to turn your life around today, by following simple, guided steps, then you've hit the jackpot.

Click here to check out the rest of 'How To Be Mindful Of Thoughts: Steps To Achieving Mindfulness And Living In The Moment (Buddha on the Inside Book 3)': www.mikemccallister.com/books

Printed in Great Britain
by Amazon